C000161508

Seven Last Words

❧

Cardinal Basil Hume OSB

Edited by Liam Kelly

DARTON · LONGMAN + TODD

First published in 2009 by
Darton, Longman and Todd Ltd
1 Spencer Court
140–142 Wandsworth High Street
London SW18 4JJ

ISBN 978–0–232–52764–3

A catalogue record for this book is available
from the British Library

Designed and produced by Sandie Boccacci
Set in 11/14pt Berling
Printed and bound in Great Britain by
The Cromwell Press Group, Trowbridge, Wiltshire

Contents

❧

Foreword

I am delighted that the late Cardinal Hume's reflections on the Seven Last Words of Jesus have now been collected together and published. These words were a source of great personal comfort in his own journey towards death. Now guided by the Cardinal's meditations they can be so for us too. The Cardinal spoke about those words on many different occasions, but now for the first time his reflections have been brought together in these few pages.

But we must not think that a book about Jesus' death on the cross is a mournful book. Yes, death is something mournful. But by the death and resurrection of Jesus Christ everything is transformed. To quote the Cardinal's own words: 'There is no Good Friday experience that does not lead to a greater understanding of sharing in the joys and triumphs of Easter Sunday.'

So the *Seven Last Words* of Jesus is really not a sad book at all. In Jesus lifted up on the Cross, we see the living sacrifice of himself, out of love for his Father. This is the gift of self, which is the heart of love, written large. In effect, it is a love story I commend for your prayerful reflection.

+ VINCENT NICHOLS
Archbishop of Birmingham

Preface

Seven times he spoke
Seven words of love
And all three hours, his silence cried
For mercy on the souls of men
Jesus our Lord is crucified

These words come from the well-known Good Friday hymn 'O Come and mourn with me awhile' written in 1849 by Frederick William Faber.

The 'seven words' refer to the last words spoken by Jesus as he was dying on the cross. These utterances are recorded in the Gospels of Mark, Luke and John, although no one Gospel contains them all.

'Father, forgive them; they do not know what they are doing.'

'Indeed, I promise you, today you will be with me in paradise.'

'Woman, this is your son.'

'My God, my God, why have you deserted me?'

'I am thirsty.'

'It is accomplished.'

'Father, into your hands I commit my spirit.'

Over 300 years ago, when massive earthquakes had devastated areas of central Peru, a Jesuit priest, Fr Alonso Messia Bedoya, prepared a Good Friday service based on the Seven Last Words of Jesus. Out of the depths of despair, he wished to show to his people that beyond the passion and death of Jesus lay the hope of resurrection. Behind the devastation and pain of the suffering of the people of Peru, too, was the hope of resurrection.

That devotion to the Seven Last Words spread and was taken up in many parts of the world, including Spain. There, in the Atlantic seaport of Cádiz, a Canon of the Cathedral commissioned the Austrian musician, Franz Joseph Haydn, to compose some music based on the Seven Last Words. Haydn produced seven sonatas preceded by an instrumental introduction, with a finale depicting the earthquake that the Gospels describe as marking the death of Jesus. The first performance was on Good Friday 1787. A single lamp shone in Cádiz Cathderal and the Bishop of Cádiz read one of the phrases from the Gospels and offered a brief meditation before Haydn's music was played. Some years later, Haydn produced his own choral version of *The Seven Last Words of Christ on the Cross*.

Today, sadly, the original sacred setting of Haydn's work has perhaps been forgotten and the circumstances behind the devotion to the Seven Last Words are almost entirely unknown. What remains with us, however, is a world still marked by tragedy, suffering and despair.

When, on 13 April 1999, Cardinal Basil Hume was told he was dying of cancer, his immediate reaction was to go to the hospital chapel to spend some time in prayer before the crucifix. He had great devotion to the last words of Jesus and he was, in a sense, making Jesus' prayer his own: 'Into your hands I commend my spirit.' Out of the depths of despair and suffering, he was searching for hope. And that is what he found in the secret of the crucifix. Three days later, in a letter to the priests of his diocese, he revealed that the cancer was not 'in its early stages', but he added: 'I have received two wonderful graces. First, I have been given time to prepare for a new future. Secondly, I find myself – uncharacteristically – calm and at peace.'

A new future – calm and at peace. Not in the depths of despair. Undoubtedly, Cardinal Basil Hume was able to draw tremendous strength from his own reflections on Jesus dying on the cross so that his own suffering became a longing for the new future.

On a number of occasions, Cardinal Hume gave reflections on the Seven Last Words of Christ. Or rather, it would appear the Seven Last Words of Christ spoke to him. Within them, he once said, there is 'a message of hope, an Easter gift which gives meaning to Good Friday's agony'. These texts are gathered here to share that message of hope in a new future. 'Let those words speak to you', Cardinal Hume wrote, 'and I will tell you what they have said to me.'

LIAM KELLY
Ampleforth
February 2009

Introduction

❧

I once sat all night by the bedside of a dying monk. The effort he made to breathe was hard, the pain was great. In the early hours of the morning, as death seemed imminent, I noticed that he was struggling to speak. I approached as close as I could to catch his words, his last words. What was it he was trying to say? A message for his friends or his family? An anxiety in his mind compounding the pain in his body? Slowly, and with difficulty, I heard the words, not always clear, it is true. But I had yet to dwell on their meaning, understand the full import of what he said. I jotted them down on a piece of paper, and afterwards … after his death and burial, I began to think about these words and heard them through his voice, a message of love and hope.

I thought of Jesus – in agony from fear and apprehension in the garden the night before he died; in pain from the flogging he had received and the crown of thorns piercing the skin of his head; in anguish because betrayed by Judas and abandoned by close friends. And now, Good Friday, after the long and painful journey up the hill called Calvary, he was crucified. Dying a most cruel and agonising death, he had still words to speak, his last words.

The last words of a dying person are precious indeed, and they are all the more so when that person is a cherished member of the family, one greatly loved and much respected. What is he trying to say? What is it that he is trying to convey, and what is the meaning of it? Sometimes, it will be a word that speaks of his suffering and pain. At other times, it will be a word of comfort, a last message to console, to be remembered and treasured. So the early Church remembered the last words of Jesus Christ, the ones he spoke as life ebbed away from him. The early Christians pondered on them, dwelt upon them, and down the ages men and women have sought, in their reflections and prayers, to find their deeper meaning. The early Christians had slowly begun to realise that this Jesus, whom they had known, was in fact the Christ, the Messiah, the anointed one, for whom they had waited for so long and whom they had so earnestly desired. But they came to see even more. This man, Jesus, the Messiah, was indeed truly God. That was a truth their minds could scarcely grasp. It was harder still when they had seen him so humiliated and so cruelly put to death. They had hoped for so much, and it had all ended in tragedy.

That sense of tragedy did not last, for the news that the tomb was empty, and the realisation that death itself had not kept him captive, filled them with joy and gave them new hope.

The Gospel recorded the incidents of his life, the things that he said and did, and this to instruct his followers and those who were to come after him, you and I among them. They wrote at length about his Passion and Death, for this had great significance for them. And they recorded his last words, the Seven Last Words. These were not just the words of a dying man, they were more. The human voice of the dying Christ was speaking to them of divine thoughts and attitudes, and as he died, amid terrible suffering, these words were not only deeply moving and poignant, but very solemn. Each of these 'last words' has the power to transform the lives of you and me, for they are the word of God. It is not possible to realise all the riches they contain. They reveal their secrets, slowly, if we meditate on them and pray. Let those words speak to you, and I will tell you what they have said to me.

1

❧

'Father, forgive them; they do not know what they are doing.'

Now with him they were also leading out two other criminals to be executed. When they reached the place called The Skull, they crucified him there and the two criminals also, one on the right, the other on the left. Jesus said, 'Father, forgive them; they do not know what they are doing.'

(Luke 23:32–4)

'They do not know what they are doing …'

They had scourged him, lacerating his body; they had put a crown of thorns on his head; they had insulted him, made fun of him. They were now nailing him to the cross. And yet in what they were doing the Roman soldiers were degrading themselves more than him. 'They do not know what they are doing' – surely their very humanity should have prevented them from inflicting upon another what they could not have faced themselves. That man should be so cruel to man – it was so then and it is often so in our own time, man's inhumanity to man. 'We do not know what we do' – that word is profound. The human voice of the Lord in his agony shows forth, here, a divine generosity which is surprising, and so very consoling. It is as if the Lord wants to go further than we could ever go to excuse us. He will find any reason to relieve us of the burden of guilt, if he can. Indeed the Roman soldiers knew no better. Their training had made them ruthless and very cruel. Of course, their actions are to be condemned: someone must be responsible and so be guilty, but these men ... 'they do not know what they are doing'. So he prays: 'Father, forgive them ...' Were there ever words so sweet to the ears of those burdened and weighed down by wrong-doing and sin?

In every human life there are things, actions and attitudes that need forgiveness; there are memories of foolishness and weakness that lurk like dark spectres to haunt us when the spirit is low or the going hard. If only we could hear, clearly and within us, that we have been forgiven. The Roman soldiers had not asked for forgiveness, and yet he asked that it should be given to them. If you and I truly want forgiveness, if our sorrow is real, what is it that stops us from knowing that we have been forgiven? Is it our failure to believe in his love for us? He loved those Roman soldiers, though they did not know him. He would not have forgiven them if he had not loved them. If we turn to him, want to love him and ask for forgiveness, we may be sure that our sorrow for the wrongs we may have done will bring us closer to him, and with closeness, peace of mind.

It is a heart-warming moment to experience forgiveness, to know again that I am loved even when I have strayed from God or done wrong. To forgive is a lovely quality in God. It is equally lovely among ourselves. When distressed by guilt or overcome with remorse, never for one moment doubt God's forgiveness. It is the faithful companion of our sorrow. And no matter what other people have done to us – the harm they have caused, the injustice they have inflicted, the ill-will they have displayed – do not ever withhold your smile of forgiveness – even when they do not know what they do.

They drove nails
through his hands
through his feet
to secure him on the cross.
He had suffered
the scourging,
thorns battered into his head
insults
humiliations
taunting,
now the pain
in hands and feet;
as the nails tore through his flesh.
The pain in his body
accompanied now
the agony of his mind,
the agony that was his
in the garden
on the night before.

And yet he forgives,
forgives them
for what they are doing
for the pain they are inflicting,
desperate almost,
to find an excuse:
'They know not what they are doing.'

Were they but obeying orders,
doing what they were told
by other men,
anxious to kill this prophet?
Can these soldiers
be excused
for their part
in so grievous a crime?
He forgives,
ignoring, so it would seem,
the question that we ask.
He forgives.
'Forgive them, Father,
for they know not what they do.'
Thus he prays.
Those words of his spoken
not from weakness
but from the strength of love

which he has for us.
There is a deeper truth
for us to learn.
It is that God seeks always
to forgive.
He will look for every reason
to forgive
to make excuses for us,
to understand.

Nonetheless he looks into our hearts
to find 'sorrow'
or at least the beginnings of it.
He expects us to be sorry,
and to say so,
to recognise the wrong
we have done.
There is comfort in remembering
    that
a humble and contrite heart
he will not spurn.

Father, forgive me; I do not know what I do. I do
not know what I have done. But, Lord, is that
entirely so? Is there not within me that uneasy
feeling in which a voice speaks, a voice difficult

to hear now because so often unheeded, a voice that speaks a reproach.

That voice calls for a response by me; not a protest, not a curse, not a cry, but a prayer, one that pierces his heart so that love may flow from it – just one word: *Sorry*.

2

❧

'Indeed, I promise you, today you will be with me in paradise.'

One of the criminals hanging there abused him. 'Are you not the Christ?' he said. 'Save yourself and us as well.' But the other spoke up and rebuked him. 'Have you no fear of God at all?' he said. 'You got the same sentence as he did, but in our case we deserved it: we are paying for what we did. But this man has done nothing wrong. Jesus,' he said, 'remember me when you come into your kingdom.' 'Indeed, I promise you,' he replied 'today you will be with me in paradise.'

(Luke 23:39–43)

If you were a thief dying in agony, at the end of a long life of crime and wrong-doing, would it be asking the impossible for you to believe in

the love of God, or in his goodness? And yet ...
the thief executed at the same time as Christ
dared to believe: 'Jesus, remember me when
you come into your kingdom.' I sense that some
of you may often doubt that God loves you and
that he wants your happiness. His absence may
be more obvious to you than his presence. You
may feel that a lifetime of sin has built barriers
that even God's love cannot scale. And yet it is
to each one of us, unless, of course, we choose
otherwise, that he will one day say: 'Today you
will be with me in paradise.' A great priest once
wrote: 'To ask a king for a trifle is to insult him.
The thief daringly asked Jesus to give the kingdom of heaven, to give it in a moment, and to
give it after a life of sin. And it was given to him
as he prayed.' And it can be so for us, too. It
needs faith and daring humility.

And so at his death he whom we call the
'good thief' knew peace of mind, forgiveness
and salvation. The other criminal had not
wanted to repent. He cursed God, and taunted
his Son. 'Are you not the Christ? Save yourself
and us as well.' We do not know what happened
to him, but the other one, the good thief, was
guaranteed, there and then, the vision of God,

the endless happiness of ecstatic love, and this right at the end of his life. He was not saved from the agony of a cruel death on a cross; indeed, like his Master he had to undergo that most cruel of deaths. But when the mind knows peace and reassurance, the pains of the body, agonising and weakening, are not strong enough to trouble the mind or rob it of its inner strength. The pain of the good thief had become the gateway to a new and richer life, the fullness of life for which we were made. Meanwhile, he stood at the threshold, waiting for the old life, with its wounds of sin, to pass as he entered into the kingdom – paradise.

And so right at the end, on his death-bed, he turned to the Lord, and was saved. That word of the Lord – 'Today you will be with me in paradise' – can be spoken to any of us, even at the last moment. It is not for us to look back in despair, not to see the past as robbing us of our future with God. Yesterday's thief can be tomorrow's saint. Our last breath can always be a sigh for forgiveness – and forgiveness is given and life with God assured.

Allow your thoughts now to dwell on those words: 'Today, you will be with me in paradise.'

But remember, too, the words: 'Father, forgive them; they do not know what they are doing.' They are addressed to us when our hearts are humble and contrite, or at least we want to be so. To know that is to experience, even now, the joy which will be fully ours in paradise.

He was suffering, too,
the good thief,
abandoned
with no family to comfort
nor friends to help.
Who remembers a common thief,
dying on a cross
for the wrong
he has done?
Who will stand by him
claim his friendship?
That thief prays
'Remember me when thou comest
into thy kingdom'.

Sad,
sorry,

repentant,
broken almost,
anxious
he sought to make amends.

The answer comes:

'This day thou wilt be with me
in paradise.'

This day –
could he have expected that?
This day –
when his final agony came
he was
at peace.
Death came
not a foe
but a gentle friend.

This day ...

A humble, contrite heart
is never spurned.
Sorrow for sin
never too late;

wrong-doing never so great
that forgiveness
will be refused.
Others may ignore,
forget, lose interest.
He never does.

He cannot forget
nor cease to wait
for that word of sorrow
for our wrong-doing,
a word that heralds
our entry into his kingdom.

Do not despair
nor give up hope,
however far
you may have wandered,
whatever wrong
you may have done,
despair must never be
a word for you.
He wants us,
wants us more
than we have
ever wanted him,

or ever could.

'This day you will be with me in
    paradise',
it will be said
to you when you have prayed
'Remember me …'.

3

❧

'Woman, this is your son.'

Near the cross of Jesus stood his mother and his mother's sister, Mary the wife of Clopas, and Mary of Magdala. Seeing his mother and the disciple he loved standing hear her, Jesus said to his mother, 'Woman this is your son'. Then to the disciple he said, 'This is your mother'. And from that moment the disciple made a place for her in his home.

(John 19:25–7)

She had been told that a sword would pierce her soul. It was an old man called Simeon who had said it to her when she had presented her Son in the Temple, as the Law prescribed. She had already known what the majority of people in our world know only too well: poverty. Soon she would learn that Herod wanted to kill her Son, and with Joseph she would have to leave her own country, and live away from home in exile. Then when her Son began his work with his people, she was in Nazareth when the villagers tried to throw him over a cliff. She sensed the opposition that grew up against him, that opposition that turned into hatred, even though many followed him and received him with enthusiasm. The officials among the religious leaders wanted to silence him. He was in danger. She feared for him.

Then his 'hour' came, that moment when he was mocked and insulted, cruelly tortured, and finally executed in a manner that was both brutal and humiliating. She stood by him, his 'hour' was hers, too, and as he suffered in mind and body she would make his agony her own. A mother makes her own the pain of a son or a daughter, and the mother's pain is more keenly felt as if in sharing it she were able to take it away from the one consumed by her love.

So she stood at the foot of the cross with the beloved disciple, John, and two or three of her friends. She had watched it all. And she saw the soldier pierce her Son's side after death, and blood and water had flowed. This was symbolising the birth of the Church, the community of those who were to believe. Her pain at this birth made her, at that moment, mother of all those who would believe, mother, that is, of the Church. 'Woman, here is your son', she heard him say as he was dying upon the cross, and he was speaking to her of John, the only apostle present, for the others had fled. Mary was to be his mother, and ours too. 'Here is your mother.' And Jesus had provided for his mother. His dying wish that John should care for her, must, surely, have been in part the healing of her sorrow.

She stands there – noble, dignified, courageous, strong. *Stabat Mater*, the mother stood. She had to be there to share his pain, to be part of his mental anguish. She was no casual on-looker, no idle spectator. She shared his pain, she was part of his anguish. Strangely, wondrously, she was again mother. His mother in his hour of need, but our mother as well. We call her mother, because she truly is, and thus she is now our mother in our time of need, calling us to be like her – dignified, noble, courageous, strong.

I have sometimes tried to comfort women who have been suffering greatly because of the loss of one very dear to them, a husband or a child. I have admired their courage – and the courage of men, too, who have been in the same situation – but I have also been able to see the utter dejection and crippling sorrow that they have had to bear, often behind the brave and dignified exterior. I have guessed that there have been tears, bitter tears sometimes, shed in secret, and uncontrollable throughout a sleepless night. What can I say? You may also have known this experience. Mary, too, knew it, as she watched her Son die so cruelly upon the cross. Her heart must have been at breaking point, even if she were able, as we are told, to stand at the foot of the cross.

'Woman, here is your son. Son, here is your mother.' John represented us all at that moment, that is those who would, as a result of the Lord's death, share in his risen life. Mary was mother, now, of the whole Church, as it was coming to birth while his life was ending. Apart from the deeper meaning of this last word it contained, too, human comfort and consolation. It was a last thought for her welfare, and the word that expressed that thought had power, surely, to heal the wound – or at least to soften the pain.

❦

When his side was pierced
blood and water flowed.
Water – its cleansing
and life-giving power
makes one with Christ,
the sons and daughters
of his Father.

Blood – shed for us,
to redeem us from sin,
given to us
to nourish and strengthen.

The Church – born from his side
as Eve from Adam –
in the waters of the font reborn,
from the chalice sustained.

Mary stood with John
with Mary and Salome, too,
a Mother mourning her Son,
suffering,
sharing his pain.

She listened to his word,
this last word

pondered it
in her heart
as was her wont,
'Woman, behold thy Son.'
His hour had come
and so had hers.
Her soul pierced
by the sword of suffering –
as Simeon had foretold –
as if in labour
she was now
mother again
Mother of the Church,
Mother of those reborn in the font
　　of baptism
and nourished by his body and blood,
the water and blood
that came from the wound in his side.

'Son, behold thy Mother.'
He took her to his own,
John, the beloved disciple,
to provide for her needs
as she would provide for his
a space for her
in his home perhaps,

most surely
a space for her
in his heart.

4

❧

'My God, my God why have you deserted me?'

When the sixth hour came there was darkness over the whole land until the ninth hour. And at the ninth hour Jesus cried out in a loud voice, 'Eloi, Eloi, lama sabachthani?' which means, 'My God, my God, why have you deserted me?'

(Mark 15:33–4)

All of us experience moments of despair and suffering. We may be sick or handicapped; we may realise that we are old and unloved, we may have been deserted or let down; we may be out of work and losing our pride. At times of great distress and confusion, thinking may only add to the pain, praying will be impossible.

Then the only helpful thing, the only possible thing is to sit or to kneel looking at the crucifix, the image of Christ dying on the cross. We may indeed have to share the darkness which was in Christ when he prayed that Psalm from the cross: 'My God, my God, why hast Thou forsaken me?' We can do no more than just look at the crucifix – but we can do no better, for then it will give up its 'secret'. It will speak to us – in our misery – of hope and of encouragement. There is no tidy, rational explanation of the crushing burden of suffering. We cannot work out easy answers about why it should be. God gave us instead not an answer but a way to find the answer … it is the cross that will reveal it, but it has to be a personal discovery. You cannot begin to see pattern and purpose unless you have known the cross and blindly let Jesus lead you from despair into hope.

That emptiness, when God is not in our lives, or so it seems, is a terrible pain. We just feel empty. The sense of being abandoned by God is the most crucifying of all pains; it is the end of hope, it is the way to despair, and to nothingness. To speak of God's love for us at such moments seems meaningless. It only adds to the pain. If we know that God is with us, there is much that we can endure, for pain and sorrow will pass and joy and peace will return. But if there is no God … or if we sense that we have been rejected … that is a crushing burden, too much for the human spirit to endure. We can only pray 'My God, my God, why have you deserted me?' The psalmist's prayer at that moment was Christ's prayer, and it spoke of the dark experience of abandonment, which was his greatest suffering. How he who was God could experience such pain, know such abandonment, such emptiness, we do not know. We can only ponder upon the fact in silent prayer. If we are called to share that same experience, and when thoughts and words increase the pain and confusion of our minds, then we are surely one with him. His darkest moment, and ours, is one darkness. Into that darkness comes his light, not ours, but given to us to be our peace.

'My God,
my God,
why hast thou

forsaken me?'
When in the mind
there is
only darkness
and fear,
when there is only emptiness
and none to help
or to console.

When life has only
death to offer
to escape from pain
and to be at rest.
Then we
cry out in anguish to God
to come to help,
to console.
When silence reigns
and no answer comes;
we are lost
abandoned,
and know only fear.

'My God, my God,
why hast thou
forsaken me?'

That prayer from the Psalm
conveys the depth of
sadness,
the anguish,
of the soul of Christ,
forsaken,
forgotten even
by God himself.
It was his prayer
as he trod
the pilgrim way,
through despair
and the dark vale
of tears and anguish
to that hope:
God's gift
to those who feel forsaken.

It is then that they must
abandon their hearts to him
when they see no point
in so doing.

A gift
when all is darkness,

emptiness too,
is precious
in the eyes
of a Father
who seeks
above all
our trusting of him
when that trust is hard to give.
Give it
and the emptiness is filled,
inner wounds healed
and peace achieved.

5

❧

'I am thirsty.'

After this, Jesus knew that everything had now been completed, and to fulfil the scripture perfectly he said: 'I am thirsty'. A jar full of vinegar stood there, so putting a sponge soaked in the vinegar on a hyssop stick they held it up to his mouth.

(John 19: 28–9)

He was parched – drained by the pain, the loss of blood and the sweating – he longed for someone to give him something to slake his terrible thirst. They gave him vinegar to drink, on a sponge stuck to the end of a spear – a bitter gift for him who had come to bring riches from God's unlimited treasury of love. It will do, so the soldiers thought. A thoughtless gesture, without some sweetness in it, is no true expression of love; it can hurt as much as Judas's kiss, an empty sign because it does not come from the heart.

But the longing in him was deeper than this. In that word 'I am thirsty', the physical reality that made him gasp for something that would refresh and comfort was the symbol of that deeper need of his, which was to give his love to all of them and to us, and to receive love in return.

Was not his greatest pain, perhaps, the pain of rejection? To be unwanted, despised, to know that others wish to inflict sadness and to hurt, and this at the hands of those who meant so much to him. So he thirsted for them all, as he thirsts for each of you and for me, and at this very moment. That word 'I am thirsty' is of all the last words which he spoke on the cross the most personal and the most intimate. It is the revelation of God's great love, at once warm and strong, for us, and for those of us also who have rejected him or despised him. We touch here upon the mystery that is the secret he would wish to share with you and with me. He thirsts for us, and, perhaps, especially for those who feel the most abandoned. God thirsts for man's love, and that thirst can only be satisfied when we have begun to thirst and hunger for him. He longs for me. He thirsts.

The psalmist prayed: 'Like the deer that yearns for running streams, so my soul is yearning for you my God. My soul is thirsting for God, when can I enter and see the face of God?' The psalmist prayed again: 'O God, you are my God, for you I long, for you my soul is thirsting. My body pines for you like a dry weary land without water.'

I long, I yearn, I thirst. Those words belong, surely, to the language of love. To long for the beloved, to yearn, to pine for the beloved – to be thirsty.

Lord, those words come hard upon my lips, for it is a language that is strange and not always mine. Do I truly yearn? Is there a pining in my heart for you? Do I thirst? Then I hear a voice that calls: *Come closer. Linger in prayer at the foot of the cross and listen, for I have a word to speak into your ear. This is my word: I thirst.* My tongue is parched – the terrible thirst of a dying man with a longing for a drink which will quench my thirst.

My heart is like a dry, weary land without

water, like a deer that yearns for running streams. So many have left me, so many have walked away. So many do not need me. Other interests, other desires have taken my place. Yet I thirst. I thirst for all of these; I thirst for you, for each one of you.

So I say again: Come closer, linger on in prayer and listen as I whisper into your ear the words 'I thirst for you'. Follow me in your thoughts and prayers, then you too will begin to long for me, to yearn, to pine, to thirst. For true love is the meeting of two thirsts – I thirst for you, you thirst for me. Then the stream runs and the land is no longer dry and weary without water, for the streams are running, the ones that flow from heart to heart.

He had endured so much;
and now the agonising pain
of hanging held only by hands and feet
his body stretched and racked.
He was thirsty,
his lips dry
his palate parched,

he longed to drink.
There was another thirst,
and from a different pain.
He had been betrayed
by his friend, by Judas.
He had been rejected by his own,
those who had supported him,
Judas, oh Judas –
betrayal hurts more
when the one who betrays
has received much
from the one he betrays –
Betrayal hurts
hurts very much.
A few days ago
they had hailed him
with palms and song.
Now they curse him,
reproach him, seemingly
hate him.

He had loved them
and he still did.
He still loved Judas
Judas who had betrayed him.

His human heart
pined for all of us
and still does.
That heart of his
revealed a divine thirst,
God's thirst for you and me.

Christ
not only man
but God as well,
speaks in human words
of realities of God
known to us
only through words and actions
which we can understand.
They gave him vinegar
a sour drink to deaden the pain.

We who can so easily betray
or at least lose our way
by forgetting or
ignoring him
who thirsts
for you and me.

What shall we give,

you and I,
to he who thirsts for us?

A sweet cooling drink –
our gift of love –
to quench the thirst
of him who first
loved us.

6

※

'It is accomplished.'

After Jesus had taken the vinegar he said, 'It is accomplished'; and bowing his head he gave up his spirit.

(John 19:30)

'It is accomplished – consummatum est.' That end was a new beginning: for him, as one day for us, the fullness of the vision of God; for us now, as it was once for him in his human nature, it is the daily carrying of the cross, and the daily rising to new life – that life hidden with Christ in God. We move now uneasily between joy and sorrow, but we know that when 'It is finished', it will be only happiness, complete and unending. There will be no more tears, only joy.

'Consummatum est' – it is achieved, it is completed. God's work has been done. 'Father, if you are willing, remove this cup from me; yet, not my will but yours be done' (Luke 22:42). Your work must be complete, your will be done on earth as it is in heaven. You sent your Son to redeem us, to free us from sin and from death, the wages of sin, to bring peace, and with peace justice. Your will was to restore in the second Adam what had been lost by the first. Was it not to restore the jungle of human misery to that paradise of happiness which was ours before sin had conquered our innocence and purity? As we watch your Son die upon the gibbet, do we see there the perfect image and likeness of you, our Father? Is this the perfection of your work? Has your purpose been achieved and your intentions brought to completion? The image and likeness of God is sorely distorted and dis-figured in the image of his Son Christ dying upon the cross. Behold the Man, Pilate had said, with irony as we would think, and here was a man 'without beauty, without majesty, no looks to attract our eyes; a thing despised and reject-ed by man, a man of sorrows and familiar with suffering, a man to make people screen their faces; he was despised ... how could we take account of him?' So Isaiah, the prophet, said. To this day the image and likeness of God will strike us thus: children distorted by hunger, men and women disfigured by torture and war, civilisation in danger of total destruction, man's greed and cruelty making of humanity something less than human, destroying life, God's precious gift, and thus denying one further finite expression of his limitless beauty. Behold the man ... God made, in Christ, to the image and likeness of man had become a thing of derision, mocked, scourged and killed. Was this, Lord, the completion of your work, the restoration of man to his original state?

The Father looked upon his Son as he was dying, and rejoiced: 'This is my beloved Son in whom I am well pleased.' No human, however distorted or disfigured, is despised or rejected by that loving Father, for his scrutiny goes to that which lies deepest within, to the mind and heart which neither sin nor death can conquer, and where true freedom is to be found, and thus love, which is freedom's power to want and so to choose. Man can fetter and conquer what the eye can behold, but the Spirit remains free and to it is given the victory. It is that inner freedom which was won upon the cross, and the reward for it is in paradise: 'Death where is thy sting' now that the Spirit has had its triumph?

The Lord has touched our human experience, and leads it now through the darkness to light, from death to life … to a life of which there is no end and where the desires of humans are finally and completely fulfilled … a happiness given to those who have sought, only and above all, that his will be done. For such his work is completed and brought to perfection.

Obedient to his Father's will
he has accomplished
the work that he was given.

To take our pain
and death as well –
upon himself.
Death the wages of sin
borne by him,
ever pure and sinless.
He had become man

[52]

to endure the pain
known by many
in wars, famine,
earthquakes too.
In the soul as well
mental anguish
adversity
loss of reason.
You know suffering?
So did he.
Have you felt abandoned?
And abandoned by God, too?
So did he.
Have you been humiliated
despised
insulted?
So was he.
You have been
misunderstood
vilified?
So was he.
He, too, walked in the dark
entered the tomb
lifeless and defeated
vanquished.

Death could not win
his body would not be imprisoned.
He rose again
victorious over death
and over sin.

He has made
all things new.
It is finished
The work is done.

There will still be
suffering,
earthquakes,
wars and famine,
mental anguish, anxiety, loss of reason
still part of human living,
but different now.
He has hidden in human pain
the seed of divine life.
Hope is now hidden in human despair
joy concealed in human sadness.
Anguish, anxiety
the ravages of war,
famines, earthquakes
hide within themselves

a rich reward
a precious treasure
life hidden with Christ in God
for the sharers in his passion.

Not for me
to read the mind of God,
nor to pronounce on his ways.
Much is hidden
little revealed.
And yet,
though hard at times to see,
love is his reason,
this
and only this
inspires his deeds.

7

❦

'Father, into your hands
I commit my spirit.'

It was now about the sixth hour and, with the sun eclipsed, a darkness came over the whole land until the ninth hour. The veil of the Temple was torn right down the middle; and when Jesus had cried out in a loud voice, he said, 'Father, into your hands I commit my spirit'. With these words he breathed his last.

(Luke 23: 44–6)

In Jesus Christ our lives, all that we are and all that we do, find their true meaning. He who became one of us, lived as we do, has made holy all that we are and all that we do, save, of course, when we sin. He has made our joys and laughter holy, our daily tasks as well, and so, too, our suffering, and also our dying. These are now holy things, sanctified because he has touched them. Human tragedies, the sorrows and pains of men, of women, of children, have been given a special dignity, and they hide within them the promise and the giving of new life. When pain is most acute, or when there is only darkness in the mind, or love is wounded, new life is born within us; it is suffering's gift to one sorely tried by pain and sorrow.

It is like the seed that is in the ground; it must die before new life can come from it. The dying of the seed is deep, hidden from view and the new life is there, too, before ever it can be seen. We do not know how that new life comes to be within us – it may be when our suffering becomes a cry to God for help; or it may be when our thoughts and actions turn away from what is evil to a life in which God's wishes become our desiring, or perhaps when we resign ourselves into his hands totally and lovingly. 'Into your hands I commend my spirit.' This was Jesus Christ's prayer at the last moment, repeated down the ages by men and women, tortured and killed for their beliefs, the martyrs. That prayer has been said by countless men and women lying sick in hospital, martyrs, too, in their way;

by parents mourning a child; by lovers broken by their parting from each other; by people tortured by anxiety and worry – by men and women of great courage and endless patience, each one of them masters of their pain and sorrow because disciples of their suffering Lord.

These are the people who have discovered, in the carrying of their cross, the secret of the resurrection – that new life comes from the dying seed. They have made themselves one with Jesus Christ in his passion and death. They share with him now that new life, the divine life, which was his when he rose from the dead, and which first comes to us when we are baptised. That divine life in us will grow, if we allow it, and it is often through pain and sorrow that this will happen. We share in his suffering and death, and discover in ours the meaning of the resurrection. There is no Good Friday experience that does not lead to a greater understanding of and sharing in the joys and triumph of Easter Sunday. Resurrection can become for each of us a daily experience. Every slight pain, every small anxiety, misunderstandings, disappointments and life's contradictions – all of these are experiences of little deaths. Our daily hurts, and every one of them, have within them the joy of resurrection. If we kiss the crucifix, we shall discover him who suffered like us and for us. That kissing can, sometimes, more easily be done, when words seem empty and meaningless. It is a way of saying 'Into your hands I commit my spirit', and often it is the best way, perhaps the only way. Relief from pain and sorrow may not be immediate; indeed we may be called to walk further carrying our cross, but the yoke will be sweeter and the burden lighter. Of course we cannot, and must not, rejoice in the pain. That would be to do violence to our instincts and to our natures. We are not made for pain; we are made for happiness. But recoiling from the cross, as is natural, we can yet rejoice in the carrying of it, but it must be for his sake, I mean to be like Christ and so with him, he in us and we in him.

The figure of the crucifix was not overcome by death. When the hopes and expectations of his friends seemed to be buried with him in the tomb, new hopes sprang forth from the midst of despair when he rose from the dead. He made all things new, suffering and death as well, your suffering and your death, too.

The end was near.
He was in great distress,
overcome by pain,
his mind in turmoil.
He had no choice
but to abandon himself
into the outstretched hands
of his heavenly Father.
His prayer 'Into your hands
I commend my spirit'
was his leap of love
from life on earth
to life with the Father.
'Into your hands
I commend my spirit.'
That was the pass word
into his presence,
into those hands,
safe hands,
stretching out
to receive
his weary soul.
Not for him
the fear of judgement,

for in him
there was no sin.

For us fear indeed.
And rightly so
if arrogance,
pride
avarice
cruelty
have reigned
and are not forgiven
because we have not sorrowed.
We can refuse
to be lifted
by those hands,
remaining self-sufficient,
steeped in evil
and empty.
Our judgement
will be swift
for we stand
self-condemned.

For those who have not turned away
but in spite of failure,
weakness and sin

have not rejected him,
we shall approach,
trembling
nervous no doubt
but reassured and at peace
as we tell the story
of our lives which only
he can understand.
He knows the burdens
we have carried,
the struggle too
the reasons for our failure
and our sins.

He whispers into our ear
'Come'
then we enter,
happy and ready
to wait
till purified
and made worthy
to be with him
and rest for ever
in those loving hands.

Epilogue

In an interview broadcast on BBC Radio 2 in 1986, Cardinal Hume revealed how important to him was the crucifix in his chapel at Archbishop's House:

'I like that because sometimes in the morning when you're tired and have a lot of worries in your head it's not easy to get the head up to God, so you have to pray with your eyes. Sometimes I just sit and look at the cross and say to myself: in all the hospitals there are people dying. A lot of people I meet or who write letters to me are suffering terribly at this moment. So, looking at the cross, I think of all those people sharing that passion, sharing the agony of our Lord. And if God became man – as indeed he did – he came to share a lot of what we all have to live and undergo and gives it meaning and purpose, and makes it holy. I find that very powerful and when people say to me: "I'm very worried", or "I've just lost my husband", or "There's been a terrible tragedy in our family – please pray for me", I say "Yes, I'll do it tomorrow morning". So sitting in the chapel, looking at the crucifix, I remember that person.'